The Redo Roo

Written and Illustrated by
Cindy R. Lee, LCSW, LADC

Cindy R. Lee, LCSW, LADC
PO Box 14060
Oklahoma City, OK 73113

The "redo" concept was derived from the Trust-Based Relational Intervention ® resources (Purvis & Cross, 1999-2015.) For more information, please read Purvis, K.B., Cross, D.R. & Sunshine, W.L. (2007) *The Connected Child: Bringing Hope and Healing to Your Adoptive Family.* New York: McGraw- Hill.

Acknowledgements:
Thank you to Christopher, Amanda and Jack for all your advice, understanding and support. Thank you to Mutte, Christie, Eric, Zachary and Emily for being a part of it all. Special thanks to Kelly and Amy Gray, David and Jean McLaughlin and the McLaughlin Family Foundation for giving the gift of healing to foster and adopted children.   Thank you to Casey Call, Henry Milton, Brooke Hayes and Jennifer Abney for all their support and guidance. Gratitude also goes to Cheryl Devoe for donating her time and editing skills to this project.

Bless you to all of you who have opened up your hearts to children from hard places. Words cannot express how grateful I am to Dr. Purvis and Dr. Cross for creating an intervention that heals.

For Gigi, Buzzy & Mutte

The Redo

Teaching Tips for Parents & Teachers by Cindy R. Lee, LCSW

Of all the strategies used to correct children, the "redo" is an all-time, outstanding, without a shadow of a doubt, favorite technique. Because it is so simple and straightforward, it's surprising that parents and teachers haven't known how to use it since the dawn of time. Yes, it is THAT GOOD! Thank you Dr. Karyn Purvis and Dr. David Cross for bringing this amazing redo revelation to the forefront. Children across the globe will benefit greatly from a "redo revolution."

Teaching Appropriate Behavior:

The goal in correcting inappropriate behavior is to obtain new appropriate behavior. We tell our children "don't do this, don't do that." We lecture, we punish, and the entire time we're using a LOT of words to make our point. We expect these words to bring about major change. It is similar to the hope we often put into the purchase of a self-help book. We buy it, read it (sometimes) and expect a major life transformation. Individuals may gain insight and information from reading the book, but the information does not magically translate into new behaviors and the death of old habits. We apply the information for a day or so, but by Friday, our old ways of functioning win out. What was read we forget and the search for the next self-help book with the "right magic" ensues. There are thousands of self-help and diet books on the market today, and people continue to buy them in search of answers. So why, with so many resources, do so many people fail to make significant change after reading a book? Because we JUST READ the words!

The bottom line is knowledge stays knowledge until we actually DO something with it! Often, we only DO something when we are accountable and have support from others who love us. Without help, we are all talk. Even though we believe what we say, the proof is in our actions. Action is hard because our brains are wired for a specific way of functioning. This wiring began before birth and has been strengthened over time by the experiences of our lives.

So what does this self-help book analogy have to do with correcting kids? When you lecture and discipline the traditional way, you offer verbal knowledge, just like a self-help book. You may get a slight change in behavior for a short period of time, but it won't last. If you want lasting change, set aside the lectures and get to the business of redoing!

What is a Redo?

A redo is just what it sounds like. A child who does something incorrectly is asked to "redo" it the correct way. Once the correct action is shown, the child is praised. As a result, a positive behavior coupled with a positive response replaces a negative behavior coupled with a punishment.

Let's say you respectfully ask your daughter to stop playing the video game and go brush her teeth. Her response is a great big "Ugh" accompanied by rolling eyes and a hard tilt of the head. She forcefully throws down the controller and heads to the bathroom, feet stomping the whole way. She may be complying with the request but not at all respectfully. In this case, the parent would ask her to do it again – a redo. We would have her sit in front of the video game while we ask again, "Please get off the video game and go brush your teeth." Once your child complies with your request WITH RESPECT then you PRAISE her for doing it the right way. Doing the right action will help her succeed and will leave you with a sense of satisfaction for helping your child learn. What a delightful way to teach. The child learns and the parent or teacher is

A Common Redo Mistake:

A common mistake caregivers and teachers make when asking for a "redo" is being too assertive when the child is dysregulated or when the child does not know what the adult is asking. If a child does not understand what to do, you must help them by showing them. If the child is dysregulated you must help them regulate. This means staying close and waiting while they self-regulate OR distracting the child with something fun for a bit to help them regulate. Then, when the child is calm, you can ask for the redo in a playful and fun manner.

The "redo" concept was derived from the Trust-Based Relational Intervention® resources (Purvis & Cross, 1999-2015.)
Purvis, K.B., Cross, D.R. & Sunshine, W.L. (2007) *The Connected Child: Bringing Hope and Healing to Your Adoptive Family*. New York: McGraw-Hill.

peacefully pleased. Time-outs, grounding and spanking have never been able to deliver that!

Do Redo's Hold Children Accountable?

Parents and teachers sometimes feel like the redo does not hold a child accountable. Not so. Remember, the goal of teaching is not to control a child or use fear to change behavior. If your goal is to control your child, you are fighting a losing battle. Controlling another human is impossible, no matter how young they are. The goal is to teach your child while staying connected so they can trust you. Once they trust you, they will TRUST that you have the ability to teach them all they need to know to become authentic. There is no room for fear in trusting relationships. Think about it - do you fear any of the people you are currently in a relationship with? If you answered no to this question, there is a reason for that. If you answered yes, do you also trust that person? Are you connected with that person? Probably not.

 Although controlling children is NOT the goal, they do need to know adults are in charge. When you utilize redos, you stay in charge, but not in a "Do as I say because I am bigger than you" way, but in a "Hey you've got talent, so let's learn how to behave so you can reach your potential" sort of way. This method is more about coming along side rather than dominating over.

Having to do something again shows 100 percent accountability and the child learns, "If I make a mistake, my parents and teachers will help me do better" as opposed to, "If I make a mistake, bad things will happen." In fact, if you make the switch from time-outs or consequences to redos, your child will be accepting at first but will likely get tired of having to redo things and conclude that sitting in a chair for a time-out was easier than learning a new skill. BUT, if you stick with it, and they redo the behavior several times, they actually master the skill and the correct response becomes automatic. Yes, really! Imagine the above scenario. When you ask your child to go brush her teeth, she

responds with "Ok mommy" and hops right up to get the job done. No counting to three, no threats, and no yelling. It's all doable with redos!

Teaching the Concept:

To teach the redo concept to your child, start by reading *The Redo Roo.* You can process the book by explaining how Roo was not in trouble when he was playing outside because he could move around freely and talk as loudly as he desired. When he gets to school, he has trouble paying attention, sitting still and staying quiet. His principal and teacher come up with a plan to help Roo behave by having him redo the inappropriate behavior in an appropriate way rather than by punishing him. After you explain the book, ask the following questions about the story to solidify learning:

- Why didn't Roo get into trouble when he played outside?
- Why was Roo getting into trouble at school?
- How did Roo's teacher help Roo stay out of trouble and solve the problem?

Just like learning any new skill, you and your child have to practice. Practicing in a fun manner when playing with your child will ensure your success when you ask for a redo. You can practice redos at home or in school by playing the Redo Role Play.

Redo Role Play with Puppets

On the back of notecards, write the scenarios you would like to practice. These would be any of the behaviors you are currently struggling with. Place them face down in front of you and your child and have the child draw one card at a time. Read the card and use the puppets to act out the scenario. Take turns playing the child role and the parent role. To ensure smiles, it is really fun to act out the wrong way first and then the right way! Make sure to stay playful and fun, so the child learns.

For more books, games and activities, please visit www.cindyrlee.com. For parenting DVD's, visit www.child.tcu.edu. Reading The Connected Child by Dr. Karyn Purvis, Dr. David Cross and Wendi Lyons Sunshine is a must!

The "redo" concept was derived from the Trust-Based Relational Intervention® resources (Purvis & Cross, 1999-2015.)
Purvis, K.B., Cross, D.R. & Sunshine, W.L. (2007) *The Connected Child: Bringing Hope and Healing to Your Adoptive Family.* New York: McGraw-Hill.

So much energy, so much flight,
Little Roo is out of sight.

He leaps above the trees so high.
He jumps up to touch the sky.

He spins fast from thing to thing.

He whirls around with so much zing.

His voice is loud. He talks so fast.
He doesn't worry. He has a blast.

He hops on rocks. He climbs a tree.
It doesn't matter. He feels free.

He plays outside all day long.
He leaps and laughs, nothing's wrong.

The day is over. It's time for bed.
He goes inside to rest his head.

He cannot sleep. He's feeling scared.
He's going to school unprepared.

When he gets there, he's distressed.
He forgot he has a test.

He zones out and daydreams of fun.
His teacher yells, "Get it done!"

So much energy, he needs to wiggle.
He needs to talk and he needs to giggle.

He chats and chats when he should be quiet.
Perhaps he needs less sugar in his diet?

He can't sit still. He's out of line.
He can't hold it in. Nothing's fine.

He needs to move. He needs to climb.
He's always stirred up at story time.

Getting time-outs are never fun.
Principal's office, here Roo comes.

Teachers are frustrated, parents are mad.
Little Roo is feeling sad.

They came up with a plan and know what to do.
They're going to teach him with a "redo."

Touching others is not ok.
He says, "Try it again, please do as I say."

"Here are some fidgets for you to hold.
Now you can sit still, like you were told."

He has success sitting still.
He's getting praise learning the skill.

Now when talking out of turn,
the teacher says, "Redo, let's learn."

He tells him to put his paw in the air.
Then calls on him so he can share.

He gets big praise when he gets it right.
He's trying harder with all his might.

If Roo doesn't hear the plans,
they do "eyes and paws" so he understands.

Once Roo hears the teacher's request,
Roo can focus and do his best.

When he's done, he gets a high-five.
Hearing "good job" helps him thrive.

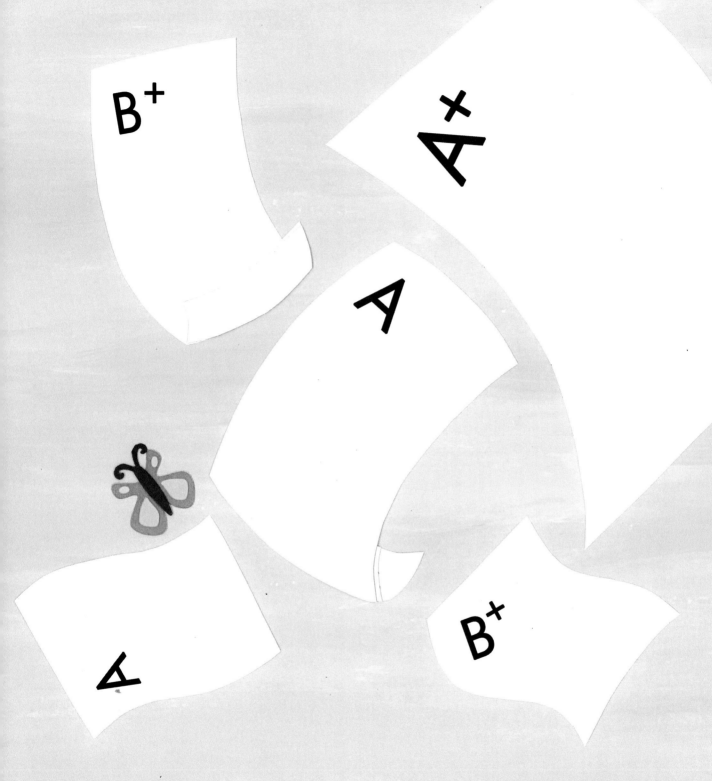

No more time-outs, frustration or yelling.
Now he can learn science, math and spelling.

His teacher helped him to self-regulate.
This is something they both celebrate.

Back at home he runs and plays.
There's just one thing he needs to say…

"You can call me the Redo Roo."
"A redo's what I like to do!"

About the Author:

Cindy R. Lee is a Licensed Clinical Social Worker and Licensed Drug and Alcohol Counselor in private practice. Cindy is the co-founder and Executive Director of HALO Project, which is an intensive outpatient program for foster and adopted children and their families. Cindy resides in Edmond, Oklahoma with her husband, children and pets.

The Redo Roo is one of eight children's books designed to teach Trust-Based Relational Intervention (TBRI) principles. TBRI was developed by Dr. Karyn Purvis and Dr. David Cross from TCU's Institute of Child Development. For more information, please visit www.child.tcu.edu.

Other Titles:

Baby Owl Lost Her Whoo teaches "Who's the Boss"

Doggie Doesn't Know No teaches "Accepting No"

The Penguin & The Fine-Looking Fish teaches "With Respect"

It's Tough to Be Gentle: A Dragon's Tale teaches "Gentle and Kind"

Made in the USA
San Bernardino, CA
08 August 2018